COLORING BOOK
GARDEN GNOMES

I0135635

JEN RACINE

instagram: @jenracinecoloring

facebook.com/jenracinecoloring

www.jenracine.com

BOOKS BY JEN RACINE

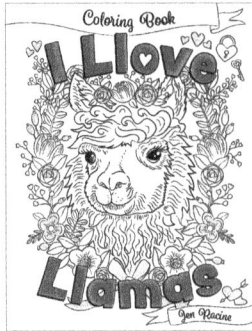

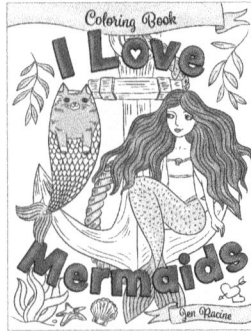

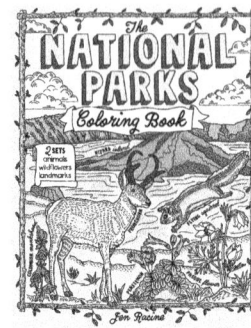

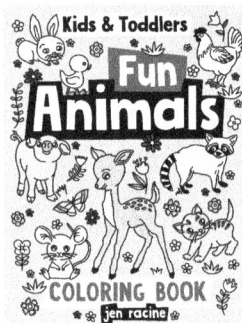

Etsy Shop
WWW.ETSY.COM/SHOP/JENRACINECOLORING

GARDEN GNOME

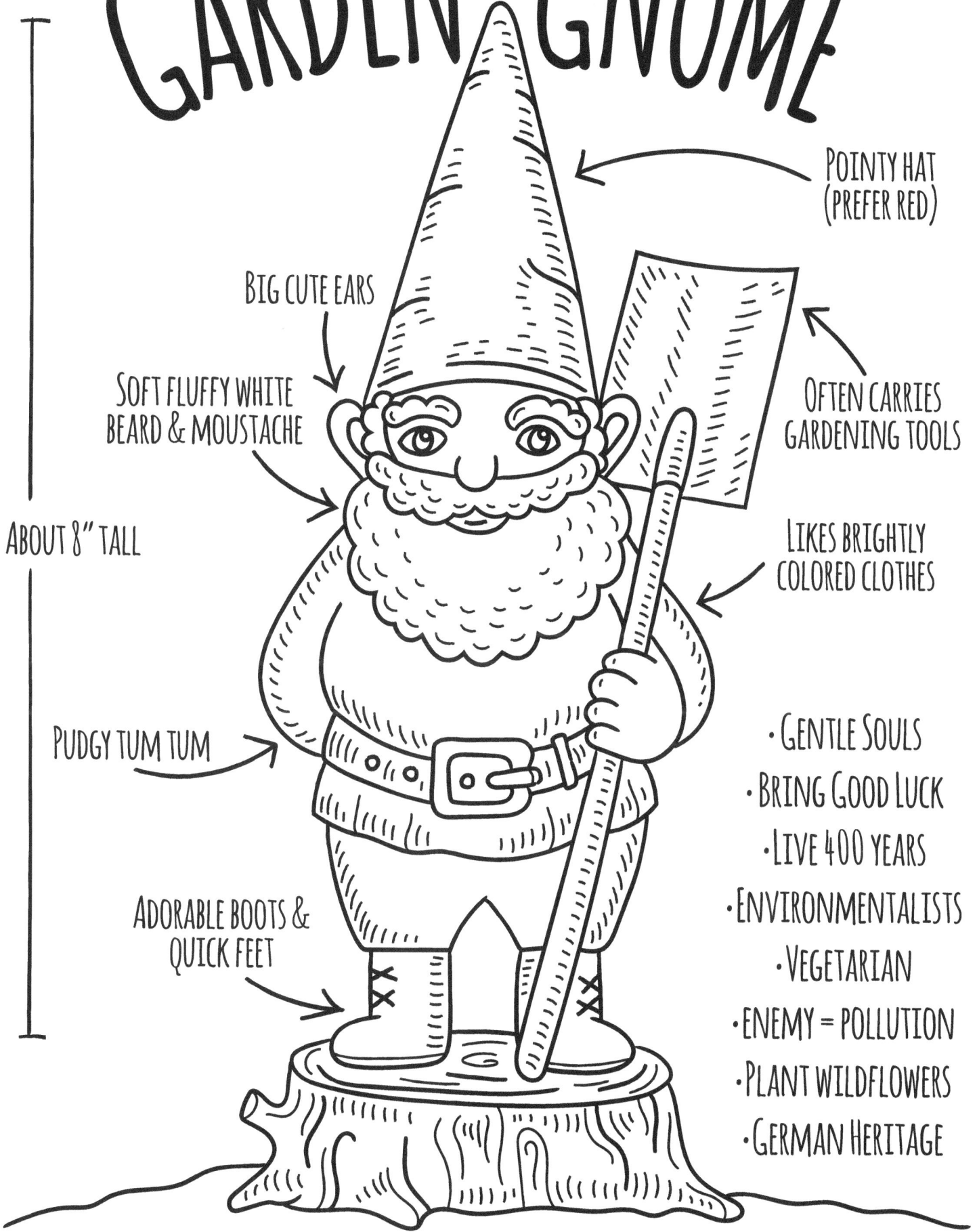

Pointy hat
(prefer red)

Big cute ears

Soft fluffy white
beard & moustache

Often carries
gardening tools

About 8" tall

Likes brightly
colored clothes

Pudgy tum tum

- Gentle Souls
- Bring Good Luck
- Live 400 years
- Environmentalists
- Vegetarian
- enemy = pollution
- Plant wildflowers
- German Heritage

Adorable boots &
quick feet

COLORED BY:

DATE:

COLORED BY:

DATE:

Colored By:

Date:

COLORED BY:

DATE:

Colored By:

Date:

COLORED BY:

DATE:

COLORED BY:

DATE:

COLORED BY:

DATE:

COLORED BY:

DATE:

COLORED BY:

DATE:

LAUGHTER IS the BEST MEDICINE

GARDEN GNOME

About 8" tall

Pointy hat
(prefer red)

Big cute ears

Soft fluffy white
beard & moustache

Often carries
gardening tools

Likes brightly
colored clothes

Pudgy tum tum

Adorable boots &
quick feet

- Gentle Souls
- Bring Good Luck
- Live 400 years
- Environmentalists
- Vegetarian
- enemy = pollution
- Plant wildflowers
- German Heritage

COLORED BY:

DATE:

COLORED BY:

DATE:

COLORED BY:

DATE:

COLORED BY:

DATE:

COLORED BY:

DATE:

COLORED BY:

DATE:

COLORED BY:

DATE:

COLORED BY:

DATE:

COLORED BY:

DATE:

COLORED BY:

DATE:

COLORED BY:

DATE:

COLORED BY:

DATE:

COLORED BY:

DATE:

COLORED BY:

DATE:

COLORED BY:

DATE:

COLORED BY:

DATE:

COLORED BY:

DATE:

LAUGHTER IS the BEST MEDICINE

COLORED BY:

DATE:

www.ingramcontent.com/pod-product-compliance
Lightning Source LLC
Chambersburg PA
CBHW080601030426
42336CB00019B/3292